ALEX ANTONIN

# Healthy mind Healthy life

*Daily practice and simple steps to improve your well-being*

# Contents

# Introduction

Mental health is a vital component of overall well-being, yet it is often overlooked or misunderstood. Just as physical health requires attention and care, so too does mental health. In today's fast-paced and often stressful world, it can be easy to neglect our mental and emotional well-being, leading to issues that affect our daily lives, relationships, and even physical health.

This guide aims to provide practical tips and methods to improve mental health, making it more accessible for everyone to take charge of their well-being. From understanding the basics of mental health to exploring practical strategies for improvement, the following sections will offer valuable insights and tools that can be integrated into everyday life.

# 1

# Understanding Mental Health

Defining Mental Health

Mental health encompasses our emotional, psychological, and social well-being. It affects how we think, feel, and act, influencing everything from our relationships to our decision-making and stress management. Mental health is not just the absence of mental illness; it's about maintaining a balanced and fulfilling life.

Common Mental Health Issues

Mental health issues can vary widely in severity and impact. Some of the most common include:

• Anxiety Disorders: Characterized by excessive fear or worry, anxiety disorders can manifest in various forms, such as generalized anxiety disorder, panic disorder, and social anxiety disorder.

• Depression: A pervasive feeling of sadness or a lack of interest in activities once enjoyed. Depression can affect sleep, appetite, energy levels, and overall mood.

• Stress: A natural response to challenges or demands, but chronic stress can lead to mental and physical health problems if not managed effectively.

• Bipolar Disorder: Involves extreme mood swings, including episodes of depression and mania or hypomania.

• Obsessive-Compulsive Disorder (OCD): Characterized by unwanted repetitive thoughts (obsessions) and/or actions (compulsions).

The Impact of Mental Health on Daily Life

Mental health significantly impacts every aspect of life. Poor mental health can lead to difficulties in concentrating, decision-making, and interacting with others. It can also manifest physically, contributing to chronic pain, fatigue, and a weakened immune system. On the other hand, good mental health can enhance resilience, improve relationships, and lead to a more fulfilling life.

# 2

# Practical Tips for Improving Mental Health

a. Establishing a Routine

Routines provide structure and a sense of control in our lives, which can be particularly beneficial for mental health. By creating a daily schedule that includes time for work, relaxation, exercise, and social activities, you can reduce uncertainty and anxiety. Routines also help to ensure that important self-care practices, such as eating well and getting enough sleep, are prioritized.

Tips for Establishing a Routine:

- Start Small: Begin by adding a few activities to your day, such as a morning walk or regular meal times.
- Be Consistent: Try to stick to the same routine each day to help your body and mind adjust.
- Include Breaks: Ensure that you have downtime to relax and unwind.

b. Exercise and Physical Activity

Exercise is a powerful tool for improving mental health. Regular physical activity releases endorphins, which are natural mood lifters. It can also reduce stress, anxiety, and symptoms of depression, while improving self-esteem and cognitive function.

Tips for Incorporating Exercise:

- Find an Activity You Enjoy: Whether it's jogging, swimming, yoga, or dancing, choose something that feels fun rather than a chore.
- Set Realistic Goals: Start with small, manageable exercise goals and gradually increase the intensity or duration.
- Make it Social: Exercising with a friend or joining a group can increase motivation and make the experience more enjoyable.

c. Healthy Eating Habits

Nutrition plays a crucial role in mental health. A balanced diet that includes a variety of nutrients can positively influence brain function and mood. Omega-3 fatty acids, antioxidants, vitamins, and minerals all contribute to mental well-being.

Tips for Healthy Eating:

- Eat Regularly: Avoid skipping meals, as this can lead to irritability and fatigue.
- Incorporate a Variety of Foods: Include plenty of fruits, vegetables, whole grains, and lean proteins in your diet.
- Limit Processed Foods: High-sugar and high-fat processed foods can lead to mood swings and decreased energy.

d. Sleep Hygiene

Good sleep is foundational for mental health. Poor sleep can exacerbate stress, anxiety, and depression, while adequate rest helps to repair and rejuvenate the body and mind.

Tips for Better Sleep:

- Establish a Bedtime Routine: Go to bed and wake up at the same

time each day, even on weekends.
- Create a Relaxing Environment: Ensure your bedroom is conducive to sleep—dark, quiet, and cool.
- Limit Screen Time Before Bed: Avoid screens at least an hour before bedtime to help your brain wind down.

e. Mindfulness and Meditation

Mindfulness and meditation are practices that help you stay present and reduce negative thinking patterns. These techniques can improve emotional regulation, decrease stress, and enhance overall well-being.

Tips for Practicing Mindfulness and Meditation:

- Start with Short Sessions: Begin with just 5-10 minutes a day and gradually increase the duration.
- Focus on Breathing: Pay attention to your breath as a simple way to stay grounded.
- Use Guided Meditations: Apps or online videos can provide structure if you're new to meditation.

f. Managing Stress

Stress is a normal part of life, but chronic stress can lead to mental and physical health issues. Learning to manage stress effectively is key to maintaining mental health.

Tips for Stress Management:

- Identify Triggers: Recognize the situations or activities that cause you stress and address them proactively.
- Practice Relaxation Techniques: Deep breathing, progressive muscle relaxation, and yoga can help reduce stress.
- Stay Organized: Keeping track of tasks and breaking them into manageable steps can prevent feeling overwhelmed.

g. Building Strong Relationships

Healthy relationships are essential for mental health. They provide support, reduce feelings of isolation, and contribute to a sense of belonging.

Tips for Building Relationships:

- Communicate Openly: Share your thoughts and feelings with those you trust.
- Spend Quality Time Together: Make time for meaningful interactions with friends and family.
- Be Supportive: Offer support to others and be open to receiving support in return.

# 3

# Therapeutic Techniques

For those looking to improve their mental health, several therapeutic techniques can be incredibly effective. These methods are often used by mental health professionals but can also be practiced independently.

a. Cognitive Behavioral Therapy (CBT)

Cognitive Behavioral Therapy (CBT) is one of the most widely used and effective forms of therapy for mental health issues. It focuses on identifying and changing negative thought patterns and behaviors.

Key Concepts of CBT:

- Cognitive Restructuring: Involves recognizing distorted thinking patterns (e.g., all-or-nothing thinking, catastrophizing) and reframing them in a more balanced way.
- Behavioral Activation: Encourages engaging in activities that align with your values and improve your mood.
- Exposure Therapy: Gradual exposure to feared situations or thoughts to reduce anxiety over time.

How to Practice CBT Techniques:

- Journaling: Write down your thoughts and identify patterns or triggers. Challenge any negative or unhelpful thoughts by asking yourself if they are based on facts or assumptions.
- Thought Records: Use structured worksheets to track and analyze your thoughts, emotions, and reactions.

b. Dialectical Behavior Therapy (DBT)

Dialectical Behavior Therapy (DBT) was originally developed to treat borderline personality disorder but has been found effective for a range of mental health issues. It combines cognitive-behavioral techniques with mindfulness practices.

Core Components of DBT:

- Mindfulness: Being present and fully engaged in the moment.
- Distress Tolerance: Developing skills to manage and tolerate distress without resorting to harmful behaviors.
- Emotional Regulation: Learning to understand and manage emotions.
- Interpersonal Effectiveness: Enhancing communication skills to improve relationships.

How to Practice DBT Techniques:

- Mindfulness Exercises: Practice staying present by focusing on your breathing or observing your thoughts without judgment.
- Self-Soothing Techniques: Engage your senses (e.g., listening to calming music, holding something soft) to manage intense emotions.

c. Art and Music Therapy

Art and music therapy provide creative outlets for expressing emotions and processing experiences. These therapies can be particularly beneficial for those who find it difficult to articulate their feelings verbally.

Benefits of Art and Music Therapy:

- Self-Expression: Allows for the expression of thoughts and feelings that might be hard to put into words.
- Stress Relief: Engaging in creative activities can reduce stress and promote relaxation.
- Emotional Release: Helps in releasing pent-up emotions in a healthy way.

How to Practice Art and Music Therapy Techniques:

- Art Therapy: Try drawing, painting, or sculpting as a way to explore your emotions.
- Music Therapy: Create playlists that reflect your mood or use music as a way to shift your emotional state.

d. Journaling and Expressive Writing

Writing can be a powerful tool for mental health. Journaling allows for self-reflection and can help in processing emotions, reducing stress, and gaining insight into one's thoughts and behaviors.

Types of Journaling:

- Gratitude Journaling: Focus on positive aspects of your life by writing down things you're thankful for.
- Expressive Writing: Write freely about your thoughts and feelings, without worrying about grammar or structure.
- Goal-Setting Journaling: Record your goals and track your progress towards achieving them.

Tips for Journaling:

- Consistency is Key: Try to write regularly, whether daily or weekly.
- Be Honest: Let your true feelings and thoughts flow without self-censorship.
- Use Prompts: If you're unsure where to start, use prompts like "What are you feeling right now?" or "What are three things that made you smile today?"

# 4

# Seeking Professional Help

While self-help strategies are valuable, there are times when seeking professional assistance is necessary for managing mental health issues.

When to Seek Professional Help

Consider reaching out to a mental health professional if you experience:

- Persistent feelings of sadness, anxiety, or hopelessness
- Difficulty functioning in daily life
- Thoughts of self-harm or suicide
- Struggles with substance abuse
- Major life changes or traumatic events that feel overwhelming

Types of Mental Health Professionals

- Psychologists: Trained in assessing and treating mental health disorders through therapy.
- Psychiatrists: Medical doctors who can diagnose mental health

conditions and prescribe medication.

- Therapists/Counselors: Provide talk therapy and can specialize in various approaches, such as CBT or DBT.
- Social Workers: Help connect individuals to resources and provide counseling and support.

How to Find a Therapist or Counselor

- Referrals: Ask for recommendations from your primary care doctor, friends, or family members.
- Online Directories: Websites like Psychology Today or Therapy Finder can help locate professionals in your area.
- Teletherapy: Consider online therapy options if in-person sessions are not feasible.

5

# The Role of Community and Support Systems

Strong social connections are crucial for mental health. Being part of a community or having a support system can provide emotional support, reduce feelings of loneliness, and increase resilience during difficult times.

Importance of Social Connections

- Emotional Support: Having people to talk to about your feelings can reduce stress and provide comfort.
- Shared Experiences: Being with others who have similar experiences can help you feel understood and less alone.
- Increased Happiness: Strong relationships are associated with higher levels of happiness and life satisfaction.

Support Groups and Online Communities

- Support Groups: These groups bring together people who are dealing with similar issues, providing a space to share experiences and advice.

- Online Communities: Virtual forums and social media groups can offer support, especially if in-person groups are not available.

Tips for Building and Maintaining Support Systems:

- Be Open: Share your thoughts and feelings with those you trust.
- Reach Out: Don't hesitate to initiate contact with friends or family, especially during tough times.
- Join Groups: Consider joining clubs, organizations, or community groups that align with your interests.

# 6

# Long-Term Strategies for Mental Wellness

Mental health is a lifelong journey that requires ongoing attention and care. Long-term strategies for maintaining mental wellness involve setting realistic goals, being proactive in managing stress, and staying connected to your support systems.

Setting Realistic Goals

Setting and achieving goals can boost self-esteem and provide a sense of purpose. However, it's important to set realistic and attainable goals to avoid unnecessary stress or disappointment.

Tips for Goal Setting:

- Be Specific: Define your goals clearly and break them into smaller, manageable steps.
- Set Time frames: Give yourself a deadline to create a sense of urgency and motivation.
- Celebrate Achievements: Acknowledge your progress, no matter how small, to keep yourself motivated.

Maintaining Mental Health Over Time

- Regular Self-Check-Ins: Periodically assess your mental health by asking yourself how you're feeling and if there are areas that need attention.
- Continue Learning: Stay informed about mental health and self-care practices through books, courses, or workshops.
- Stay Flexible: Life changes, and so do your mental health needs. Be open to adjusting your strategies as necessary.

Preventing Relapse or Setbacks

- Identify Triggers: Be aware of situations or behaviors that may lead to a decline in mental health and develop strategies to manage them.
- Build Resilience: Focus on developing skills like problem-solving, adaptability, and positive thinking to cope with challenges.
- Seek Support Early: Don't wait for a crisis to seek help—reach out when you first notice signs of distress.

# 7

# Conclusion

Maintaining mental health is an ongoing process that requires awareness, effort, and a proactive approach. By understanding what mental health entails and employing practical strategies such as establishing routines, seeking support, and practicing mindfulness, individuals can significantly improve their emotional and psychological well-being.

Remember, mental health is just as important as physical health, and taking steps to nurture it can lead to a more balanced, fulfilling life. Whether through self-help methods or seeking professional assistance, prioritizing mental health is a powerful step towards overall wellness.

It's important to be kind to yourself during this journey. Progress may be gradual, and setbacks are normal, but each step you take towards better mental health is valuable. Keep moving forward, and don't hesitate to reach out for support when you need it. You're not alone in this—resources, communities, and professionals are available to help guide you on your path to mental well-being.

1. American Psychological Association. (n.d.). Mental health resources. Retrieved August 6, 2024, from https://www.apa.org/topics/mental-health

2. National Institute of Mental Health. (n.d.). Mental health information. Retrieved August 6, 2024, from https://www.nimh.nih.gov/health/topics/index.shtml

3. Mayo Clinic. (n.d.). Mental health. Retrieved August 6, 2024, from https://www.mayoclinic.org/healthy-lifestyle/adult-health/in-depth/mental-health/art-20044098

4. Mindful.org. (n.d.). Mindfulness-Based Stress Reduction (MBSR). Retrieved August 6, 2024, from https://www.mindful.org/what-is-mindfulness/

5. National Alliance on Mental Illness. (n.d.). Mental health conditions. Retrieved August 6, 2024, from https://www.nami.org/About-Mental-Illness/Mental-Health-Conditions

6. Beck, A. T. (2011). Cognitive therapy: Basics and beyond. Guilford Press.

7. Leahy, R. L. (2003). Cognitive therapy techniques: A practitioner's guide. Guilford Press.

8. World Health Organization. (n.d.). Mental health: Strengthening our response. Retrieved August 6, 2024, from https://www.who.int/news-room/fact-sheets/detail/mental-health-strengthening-our-response

9. Psychology Today. (n.d.). Find a therapist. Retrieved August 6, 2024, from https://www.psychologytoday.com/us/therapists